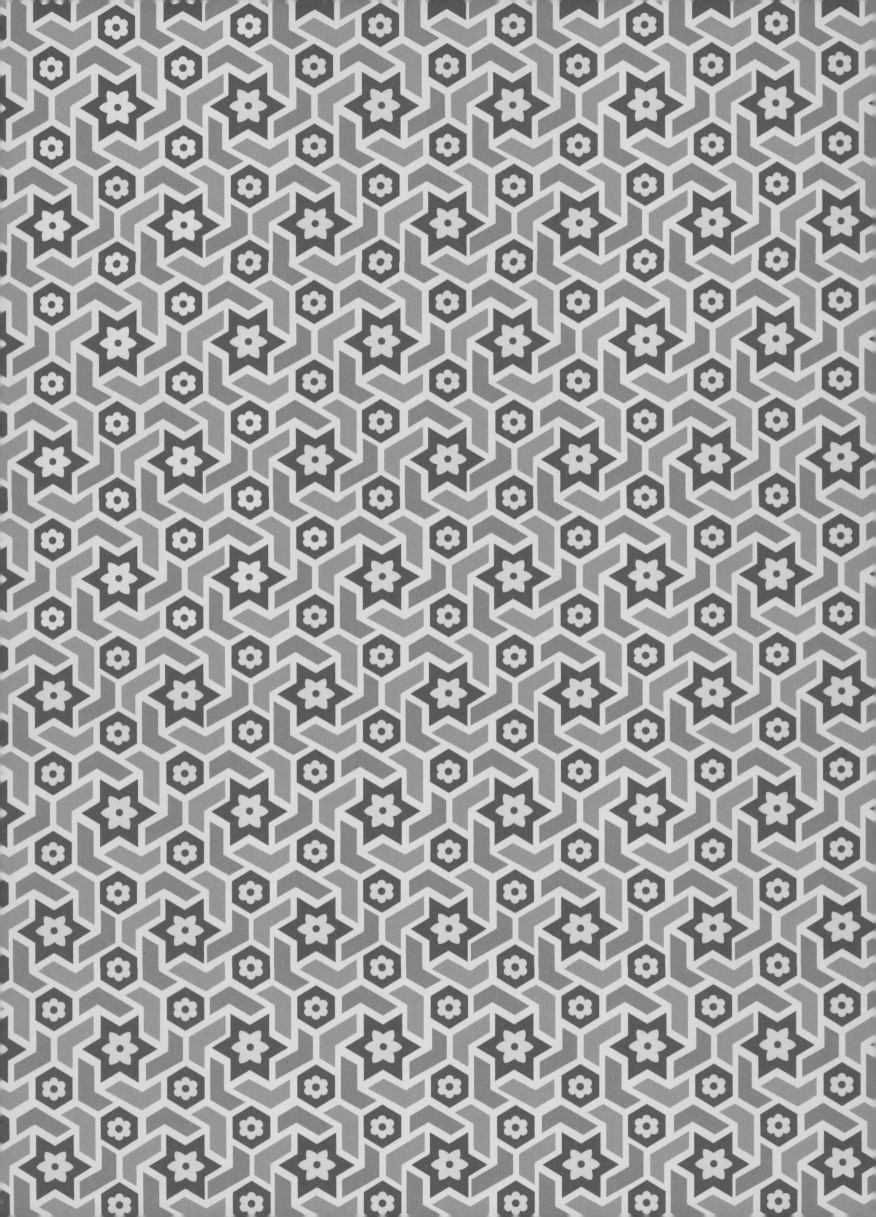

HOW THE
NEW
SEVEN
WONDERS
OF THE WORLD WERE
BUILT

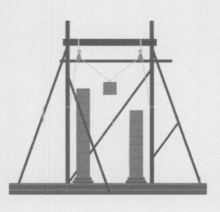

Albatros

Contents

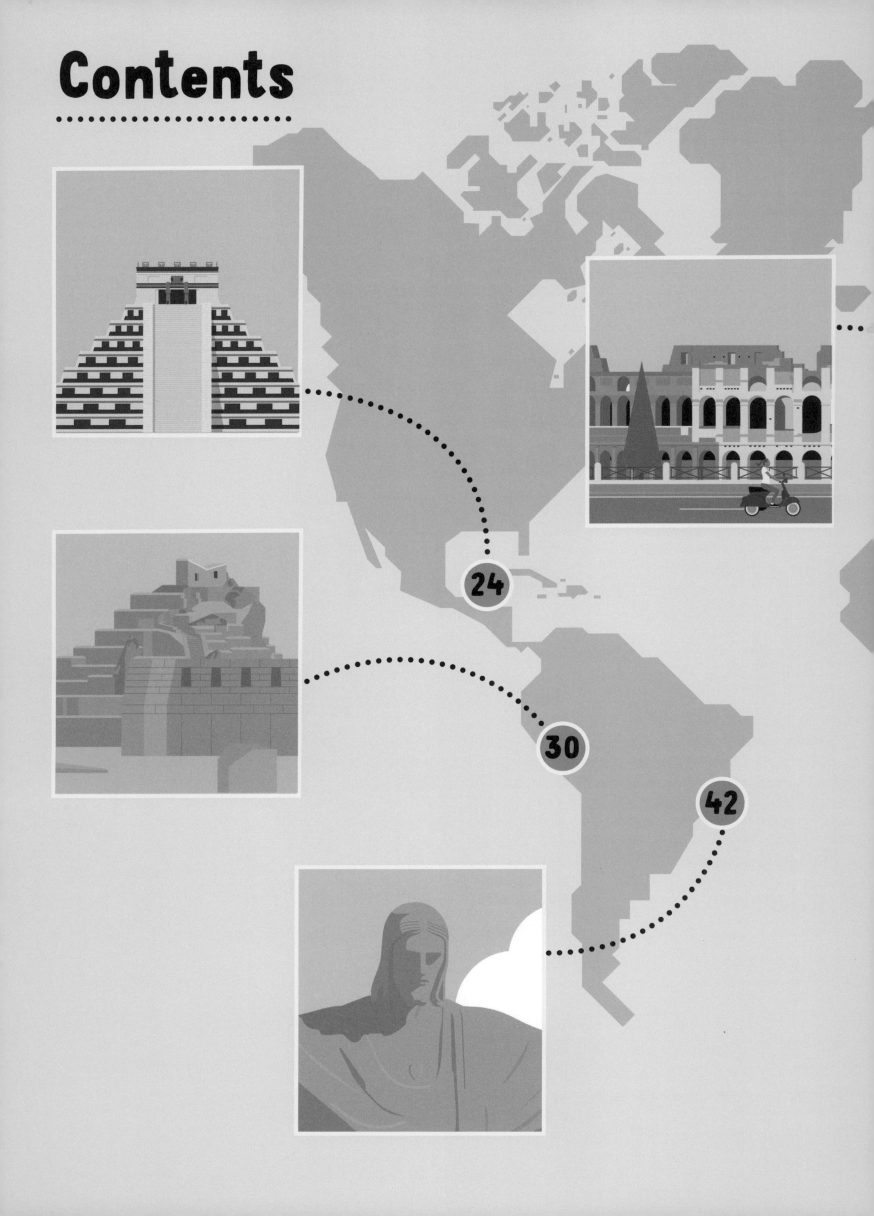

18

12

36

6

Introduction

Just like us (the authors), you (the readers) are surely fascinated by these buildings. Even history and architecture buffs, who create different lists of the wonders of the world, are fascinated. There are many such lists, but the official list of the New Seven Wonders of the World was created between 2000 and 2007, when the Swiss-based New7Wonders Foundation compiled the list with the help of online voting. Visitors to the site chose from 176 candidates, and on July 7, 2007, an official list of the New Seven Wonders of the World was announced. Over 600 million voters selected the seven winners, which we're about to learn more about.

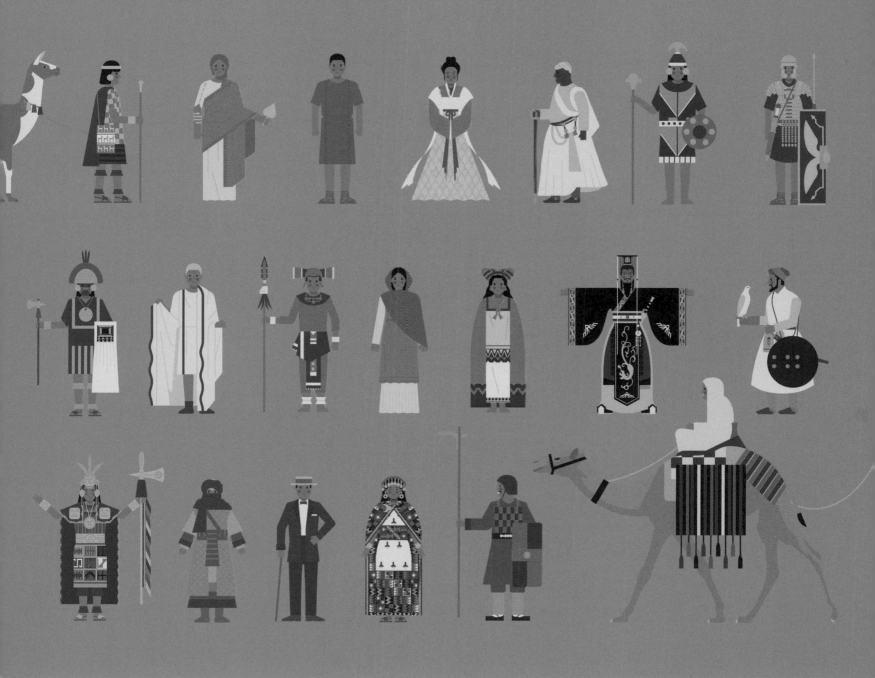

Worldview

The first list of the wonders of the world began to appear way back in antiquity, but the Seven Wonders of the Ancient World were not finalized until the Renaissance, sometime around the 15th century. Only one wonder from this classic list still exists, and as it turns out, it is also the oldest: the Pyramids of Giza. Our understanding of the other wonders is a little hazy. And we know even less about how they were built than we do about what they looked like. But we do know something. Thanks to modern research and historical research, we have a sense of how these monuments were built.

How Wonders Are Made

One advantage of this book is that all the new wonders, although many of them look differently than they originally did, are still standing. We have therefore tried to portray the wonders as they probably looked at the time of their creation. For the construction methods, we focus on specific details typical of the selected building. So, without any further ado, please join us in this journey through time.

The New Seven Wonders

More than two thousand years have passed since the creation of the first rankings of the Wonders of the World. Since then, many other impressive buildings have been built. The new wonders of the world thus show us how architecture developed both historically and globally. And they allow us to better understand the lives of those who built the New Wonders of the World, as well as those they were built for.

The Great Wall of China

It is called the Great Wall of China mainly in America and Europe. In China, it is more precisely called the Long Wall. Measuring the wall is quite difficult, but counting all the bends and breaks, it is a staggering 13,170 miles.

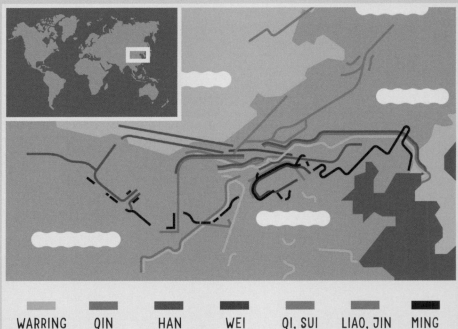

| WARRING STATES | QIN | HAN | WEI | QI, SUI | LIAO, JIN | MING |

HISTORICAL PERIODS

Timeline

Construction on the Great Wall dates back to the 7th century BCE, back during the period of the Warring States. When this period ended, the states joined together to form China. The main building of the wall dates back to the first Qin dynasty, around 210 BCE. During the Han dynasty in the 1st century BCE and during the Jin Empire (1138–1198), construction took place on the fortifications north of today's Great Wall of China, at the boundary of Outer and Inner Mongolia. The last period of construction was during the Ming dynasty (1368–1644).

Emperor

The complex of the original defensive walls from the 3rd century BCE gradually grew to prevent raids from marauding tribes. The first emperor to connect the defensive walls was Qin Shi Huang, founder of the Qin dynasty. However, the wall acquired its current form only during the Ming dynasty in the 14th–17th centuries.

EMPEROR
QIN SHI HUANG

Meng Tian

A wide range of builders and architects took part in the construction, but one of the few prominent names to withstand the test of time is Meng Tian, a major Qing dynasty general who personally managed and led the work on the wall.

GENERAL MENG TIAN

Building Method

At first, the earthen structure was probably built using wooden beams. It was gradually replaced by more durable materials of stone and of fired and unfired bricks. The type of stone depended on the local landscape. The foundations were built of large stone blocks or the building was based on a solid rocky subsoil. The building methods differed, but we can generally say that an earthen construction was first built from gradually packed-down layers of soil and stones. It was placed between wooden walls or a reinforced wooden or reed grate. Then the side walls were lined with stones or bricks.

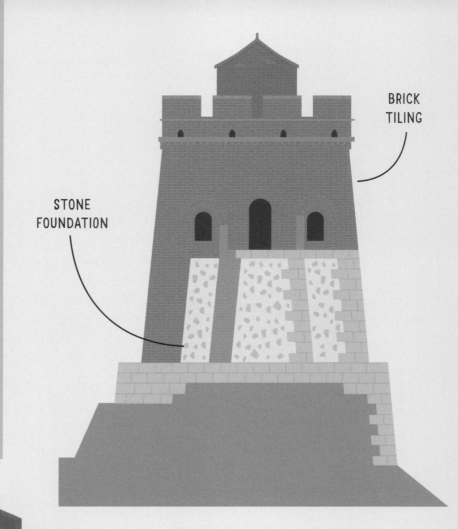

BRICK TILING

STONE FOUNDATION

GUARD POST

Thousands of Towers

The total number of towers is estimated to be about 25,000. At larger intervals, barracks, supply warehouses, headquarters, and fortresses were built. To transmit messages about the movement of the enemy, guard patrols used smoke or light signals.

CROSS SECTION OF THE TOWER

THE TOWERS HAD SEVERAL FLOORS

Ming Dynasty

The wall acquired today's form during the Ming dynasty, when it was rebuilt on an even larger scale using durable materials. The Ming dynasty was a time of development and prosperity. Irrigation systems were built, cotton was grown, and silk and porcelain were made. This period was the last national Chinese dynasty before the conquest of the Manchurian Qing Empire in 1644. After the fall of the Qing Empire in 1912, the Republic of China was founded.

PORCELAIN

FLAG OF THE MING DYNASTY

WOMEN'S CLOTHING FROM THE MING DYNASTY

DETAIL OF THE MASONRY

Who Built the Wall?

For such a monumental project, a diverse group of people worked on the construction site. In the first phase, they were mainly peasants. Emperor Qin Shi Huang enslaved and imprisoned several million citizens of the empire, forcing them to work on the wall. Later, during the Ming dynasty, this task was entrusted to soldiers and skilled craftsmen who received payment for their work.

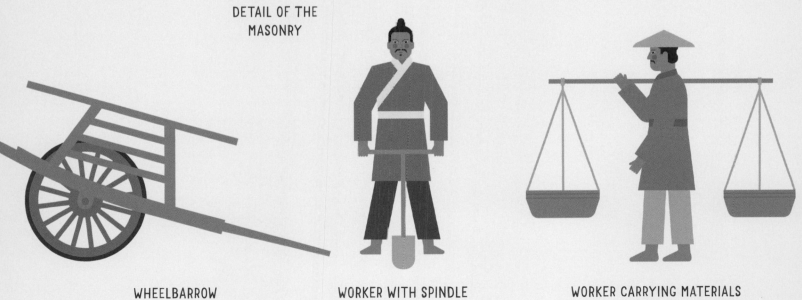

WHEELBARROW

WORKER WITH SPINDLE

WORKER CARRYING MATERIALS

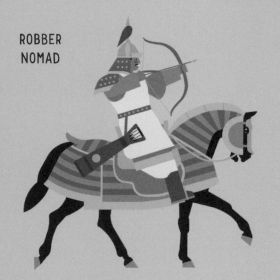

ROBBER
NOMAD

The Advantages of the Terrain

The Great Wall often uses the landscape to have stronger defenses, which is why it often leads along mountain ridges in remote terrain. The wall was not intended to repel a massive attack by enemy troops, but rather to make it difficult for nomadic tribes to raid the interior of the empire.

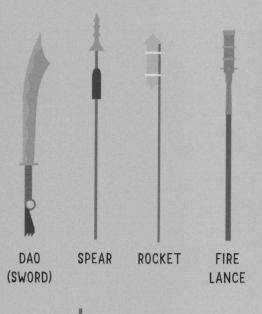

DAO
(SWORD) SPEAR ROCKET FIRE
LANCE

CHINESE
SOLDIER

Badaling

This section, the most famous one, is very easy to get to from the metropolis of Beijing. The ascent is not too difficult either. However, it is necessary to prepare for the crowds of tourists and vendors.

Simatai

Although such extensive renovations have not taken place in this section, it has both ruins and parts that are intact. Many fans from China and abroad consider it the best stretch of the entire Great Wall. While the eastern part requires visitors to be more physically fit, the western part is a lot easier to climb. You will rarely come across tourists here.

Mutianyu

After Badaling, this is the second best-maintained section of the wall. It is surrounded by forest and offers beautiful views of the surrounding countryside in the summer and fall.

Petra

Petra is a Greek word meaning "rock." It is also the name an ancient rock town and burial ground and a current archeological site of the Nabataean Kingdom in modern-day Jordan.

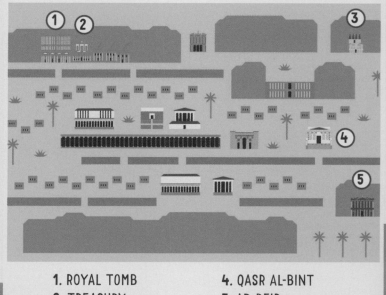

1. ROYAL TOMB
2. TREASURY
3. OBELISK TOMB
4. QASR AL-BINT
5. AD-DEIR

ROYAL TOMB

TREASURY

TRADITIONAL WOMEN'S CLOTHING

NABATEAN WARRIOR

12

Rock City

According to legend, Moses led the tribes of the Israelites, who were thirsty from a water shortage in the dry desert. So, he struck a rock with his staff and out of the rock gushed drinking water. Real-world springs like these served as a reservoir water for the city, thanks to an ingenious system of inflow channels, along with cisterns and tanks.

Oasis

Petra was the only place in this inhospitable landscape at the crossroads of routes that could provide caravans with supplies and refuge. Oases, as such places are called, make Petra a green city in the middle of an arid sandy desert, thanks to springs and reservoirs.

The Nabateans

Originally a nomadic tribe, the Nabataeans settled in the area before the 4th century BCE. Given the strategic location of land lying on several important trade routes connecting Egypt, the Mediterranean, India, and China, the Nabataeans soon became traders.

Caravan

A caravan is a group of people, accompanied by animals, who travel for a specific reason like trading or moving. In this case, they were traders traveling on camels accustomed to life in the desert.

SANDSTONE CHANGES COLOR DEPENDING ON THE TIME OF DAY.

CARVED PORTRAITS OF NABATAEAN DEITIES ARE CALLED BETYLS. THIS ONE IS THE GODDESS OF HAYYAN

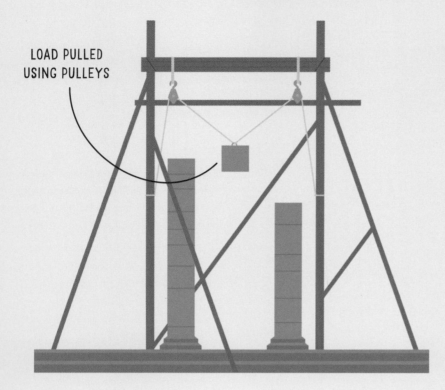

LOAD PULLED
USING PULLEYS

COLONNADE
RECONSTRUCTION

Scaffolding or climbing?

The exact construction process for the building is unknown. It is possible that the builders used wooden scaffolding, even though wood was a rare commodity in the area. According to one theory, the workers, secured by a rope, climbed up using holes carved into the rock on both sides of the building. It is also possible that platforms hanging on ropes were used.

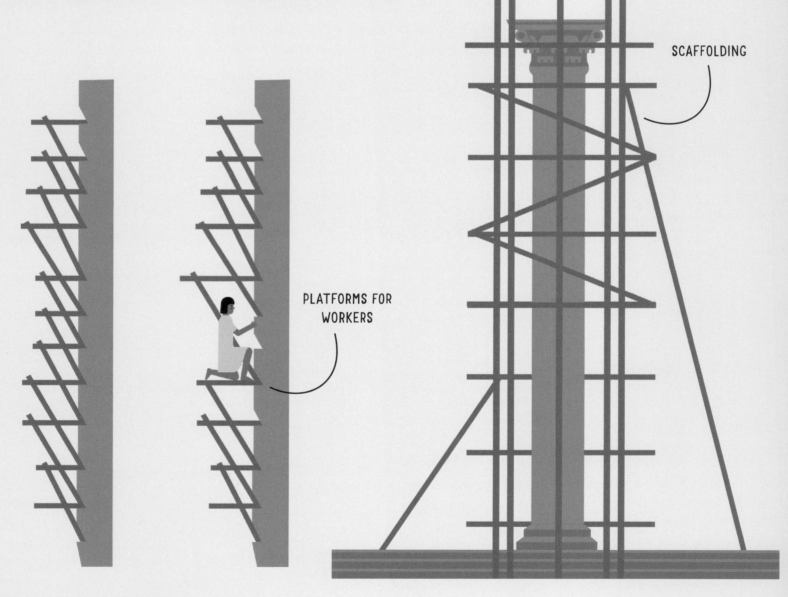

PLATFORMS FOR
WORKERS

SCAFFOLDING

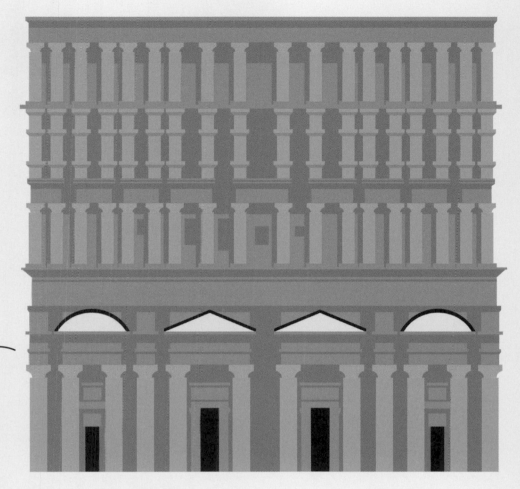

THE ORIGINAL APPEARANCE
OF THE ROYAL TOMB

Reconstruction

The first renovation took place in the 1950s. Since then, various renovations have taken place, but since the repairs have not been properly marked, the visitor cannot see what is authentic and what is inauthentic. Unfortunately, most of the buildings have been damaged by earthquakes, time, thieves, and vandals, but also by strong torrential rain, flash floods, and wind bringing in salt from the Dead Sea.

Carved City

Gauging from the materials excavated from Petra, the parts of its architecture that could not be carved were built economically, for example with a method called cantilever construction. If the stone from the carved parts were not enough, there were three major sandstone quarries for construction nearby.

UNIQUE WALL
DECORATION

Wall Decoration

On the parts of the Nabataean Monuments that have been excavated so far, there are traces of murals, especially striking for their geometric shapes, which required precise planning. Murals from this time show no comparable geometric design. Their uniqueness thus helps us decipher the history of the city and its inhabitants.

Tombs

When you follow in the footsteps of ancient caravans and walk through a gorge called Siq, just before the end you will discover the first of two monumental tombs. The first is called Al-Khazneh (Treasury). The second tomb high in the mountains is Ad-Deir (the Monastery). It is similar to the Treasury, but its dimensions still surpass it. Their façades—over 13 stories high!—are carved into sandstone and bear signs of Greek architecture.

Obelisk Tomb

The first Nabataean tomb, which is still standing before you enter the gorge, dates from the 1st century BCE. Because of the two different architectural styles, used at the same time, the tomb looks like two buildings. The designation "obelisk" is inaccurate, though. Although the columns may resemble obelisks (monuments), they are actually so-called "nefeshot" (singular "nefesh"), which are basically tombstones carved into the rock with the name of the deceased carved into the base of the column.

PROBABLE APPEARANCE OF AD-DEIR

PROBABLE
APPEARANCE OF THE
OBELISK TOMB

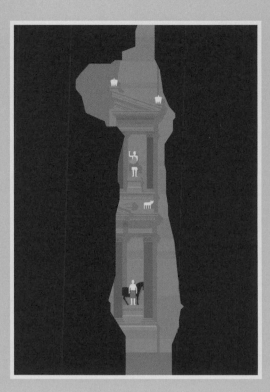

Siq Gorge

The only access road to Petra is a natural trail in the rocks that allowed the Nabataeans to protect access to the city. On the side of the gorge are channels through which water was supplied to the city from Moses Valley.

Qasr al-Bint

Many meanings have been ascribed to this tomb, which has been rebuilt many times, making its appearance a unique mixture of Egyptian, Greek, and Roman influences. Unfortunately, numerous earthquakes have had the greatest influence on the building, as well as on other monuments. Qasr al-Bint is Petra's best-preserved building, thanks to the ingenious use of equally large ashlar stone bricks interspersed with wooden slabs, making the building more resistant to earthquakes.

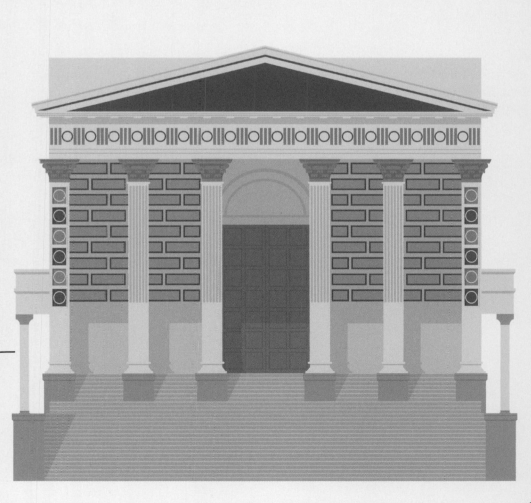

PROBABLE APPEARANCE
OF QASR AL-BINT

The Colosseum

The Colosseum in Rome—also called the Flavian Amphitheater, from the original Latin name *Amphitheatrum Flavianum*—is perhaps the most famous building of its type. Its nickname comes from the emperors of the Flavian dynasty, who built it. It is a magnificent arena that once hosted gladiator games and battle reenactments—even sea battles with sailing ships!

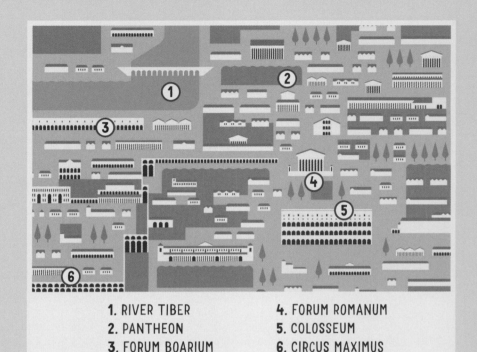

1. RIVER TIBER
2. PANTHEON
3. FORUM BOARIUM
4. FORUM ROMANUM
5. COLOSSEUM
6. CIRCUS MAXIMUS

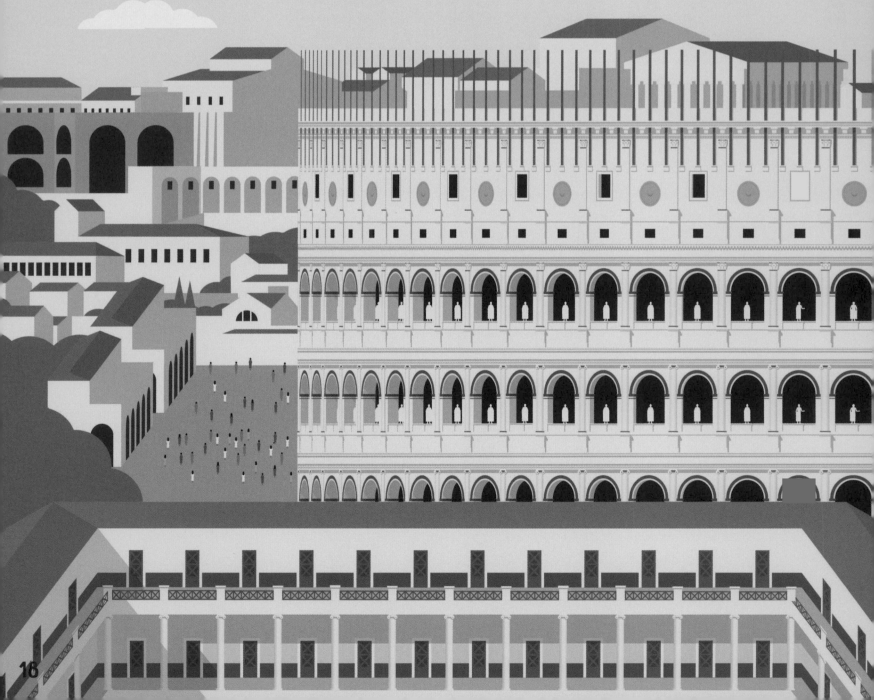

Arena

The Colosseum is an open arena shaped like an ellipse enclosed by a protective wall and surrounded by an auditorium (Latin: *cavea*). It was similar to the ancient theaters, divided into wedge-shaped sections (*cunei*). The amphitheater was intended for a wide range of events, especially gladiatorial games (*munera*), the hunting of wild animals (*venatio*), executions, mythological scenes, historical battle reenactments, and even naval battles (*naumachia*).

Seating Arrangements

There were 48,000 seats on three levels and 4,500 standing-room-only seats on the fourth level. The leading places just above the arena belonged to the elite. The highest part was reserved for commoners and peasants.

EMPERORS, CONSULS, AND SOLDIERS BELONGED TO THE ELITE OF SOCIETY, UNLIKE WOMEN AND ENSLAVED PEOPLE.

At the Bottom of the Arena

The construction of the Roman Colosseum was underway, the watery area dried out for the needs of the building. It was then filled in layers with pieces of stones and covered by mortar with *pozzolana* (volcanic ash) and strengthened by repeated pressure, called compaction.

Four ways

Minor differences in the construction have led archaeologists to think that the construction was carried out by four different contractors at the same time, each working on a separate quarter of the Colosseum.

The Crane

During the construction of the Colosseum, builders used large cranes, pulleys, and sophisticated scaffolding. Magna rota, or polyspaston, was a human or animal-powered crane that is not very different in principle from the current ones. The current ones are, of course, more complex and, instead of slaves and animals, they are powered by fuel, but both of these machines use the principle of a hoist.

BASIC SUPPORTING BRICK OF THE ARCH

CONICAL BRICKS CALLED *VOUSSOIRS*

BEARING WALL

TEMPORARY WOODEN ARCH SUPPORT—FORMWORK

BASE OF THE ARCH

The Arch

A typical feature of the Colosseum's architecture is the arch—a construction that spans openings in walls. Due to their physical properties, arches are an excellent support, as they distribute pressure and the structures are more stable.

JIB

LOWER FLOORS HAD PRIMITIVE ELEVATORS FOR GLADIATORS AND ANIMALS

PULLEYS

TREADWHEEL

THE CRANE

Tools

At the time of construction, the workers used metal and bronze tools. The tools were not very different from today's tools. Wooden handles and metal heads were the basis for the weapons of the gladiators and soldiers. Common throughout Rome was also ceramic, the main material for producing containers.

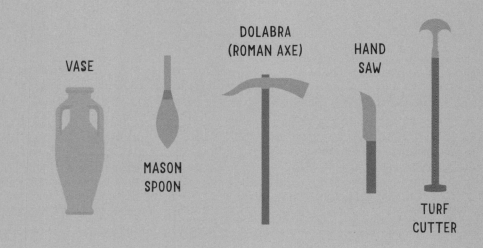

VASE

MASON SPOON

DOLABRA (ROMAN AXE)

HAND SAW

TURF CUTTER

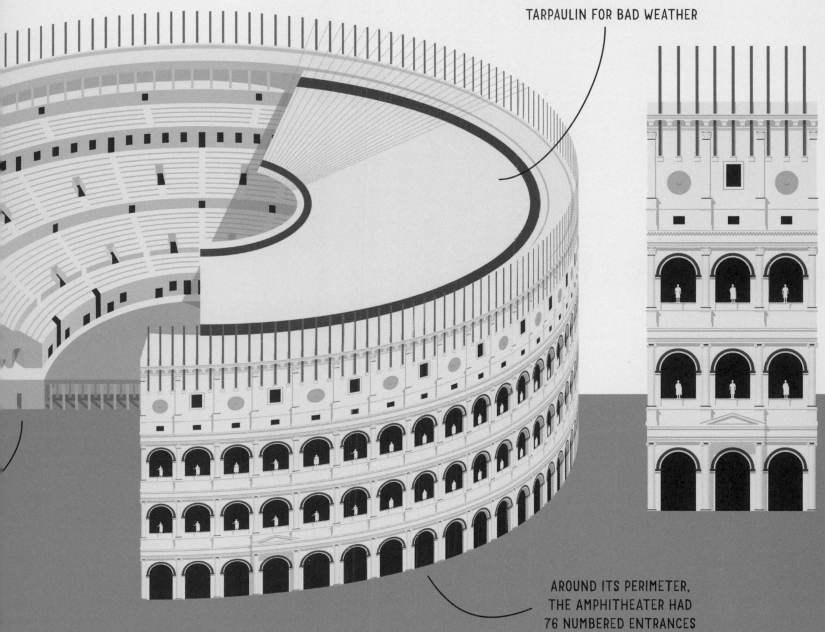

TARPAULIN FOR BAD WEATHER

AROUND ITS PERIMETER, THE AMPHITHEATER HAD 76 NUMBERED ENTRANCES

Orders

The façade of the Colosseum stands out with its superposed so-called *orders*, where the individual ancient architectural styles follow from bottom to top. On the ground floor is the Tuscan order (the Roman version of Doric). Above it is Ionian and Corinthian, with Composite on the top floor.

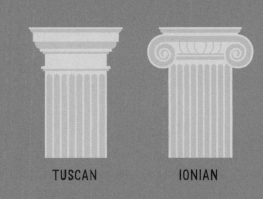

TUSCAN

IONIAN

CORINTHIAN

COMPOSITE

Emperor Nero

The Colosseum stands on the site of the original palace of Nero, called Domus Aurea (Golden House), built on a site vacated after the devastating fire of Rome during Nero's reign. People hated cruel Nero and everything connected with him. Emperor Vespasian, who had the Colosseum built, on the other hand, was very popular and did everything he could to win over public opinion. For instance, he replaced Nero's statue with a colossal statue of the sun god Sol—this "colossus" gave the amphitheater its final name.

A CHURCH INSIDE THE COLOSSEUM

VESPASIAN SESTERTIUS— ROMAN COIN

EMPEROR VESPASIAN

STATUE OF THE SUN GOD, SOL

Gladiators

Gladiatorial games, organized during the Roman Games, are most often associated with the amphitheater—where religious ceremonies, theaters, and other artistic productions were also held. Very often, different scenes, like forests, mountains, and lakes, were used to increase the effect of the spectacle.

MURMILLO

The Murmillones

A Murmillo (or "fish gladiator") was a type of gladiator whose name comes from the shape of his helmet. These gladiators had large shields and fought with short swords.

RETIARIUS

Transformations of the Colosseum

The subsoil in the south of the building does not seem to have been supportive enough, which is partly why that part of the Colosseum crashed in an earthquake in 1349. Most of the fallen stones were used by the Romans to then construct palaces, churches, hospitals, and other buildings. In the mid 14th century, a religious order moved into the northern third of the building and inhabited it until the early 19th century.

Modern History

Due to air pollution and deterioration, a major restoration program was launched between 1993 and 2000, costing over $20 million dollars. The last major renovation was completed in 2016. The entire façade was cleaned and sanitized. Further repairs are planned, including the floor of the arena and the interior of the Colosseum.

THE COLOSSEUM NOWADAYS

The Retiarii

The Retiarii were the fastest of the gladiators. Even though a Retiarius did not have a helmet to see well, his advantage was the net in which his caught his opponents. His only armor was his shoulder protection, and he often used a trident..

The Secutors

A Secutor had an egg-shaped helmet with eye holes that didn't fit as easily into the net as a Murmillo's helmet.

SECUTOR

The Bestiarii

A fighter who fought animals was called a Bestiarius. The Bestiarii were not as popular as other gladiators, and instead of armor, they were protected only by leather.

23

Chichén Itzá

Chichén Itzá, in Central America, was one of the largest and most important Mayan cities. It was not only a religious center, but was also home to 50,000 people.

1. CENOTE
2. PLAYING FIELD
3. THE TEMPLE OF KUKULKAN
4. TZOMPANTLI
5. THE TEMPLE OF THE WARRIORS
6. OBSERVATORY

THE HEAD OF THE GOD KUKULKAN

THE MAYAN CALENDAR

CHAAC—THE GOD OF THE RAIN

Discovery

Long ago, the city was abandoned, but it was never forgotten. The first extensive and detailed description was provided by British explorer Alfred Maudslay in a book in the 1880s. The first research, lasting 30 years, was then conducted by the American-born archeologist Edward Herbert Thompson.

"The Edge of the Well"

It would be possible to translate the name of the ancient city this way. "Chi" means edge and "chen" means well. Itza was the name of the economically and politically dominant inhabitants of the city. The name Itza could also be translated as magical (*itz*) water (*ha*). In the city and its surroundings, there are naturally formed wells known as cenotes. These limestone abysses are full of water and served as a reservoir of drinking water for the city's inhabitants.

THE ARISTOCRACY FROM THE CLASSICAL MAYAN PERIOD OF THE 3RD–10TH CENTURIES CE.

Cenote—A Sacrificial Well

A well that was a third of a mile away from the pyramid served, in part, as a shrine and sacrificial altar. In times of drought, the human victims were thrown 100 feet down into the well to secure the favor of Chaac: the god of rain, wind, thunder, and lightning. These wells, along with the caves, were thought to be gates to the underworld.

THE PYRAMID OF KUKULKAN

Mayan—Toltec Culture

The city was apparently founded at the end of the 5th century CE. And people lived contentedly in it for 400 years, when the city was destroyed. We call this the Classical Period. In the post-Classical Period, during the second half of the 10th century, the Toltecs arrived, led according to legend by the god Kukulkan—a feathered snake also known as Quetzalcoatl.

NOBLEWOMAN

NOBLEWOMAN

RULER

WARRIOR

The Pyramid of Kukulkan

The grand centerpiece of the city is Kukulkan's Pyramid. Comprised of nine terraces, it measures 80 feet high. Four staircases at 45-degree angles are arranged in the four cardinal directions: north, south, east, and west. Along with the upper platform, they have the same number of stairs as the days of the year, and they lead to the top of the temple.

Construction Method

The structures were built on stone foundations, often in the shape of pyramids, formed by a mixture of stones and lime mortar. These foundations were then sheathed at the very end with a thick stone layer. The buildings were created in layers, and each floor was separated by walls into spaces of various sizes.

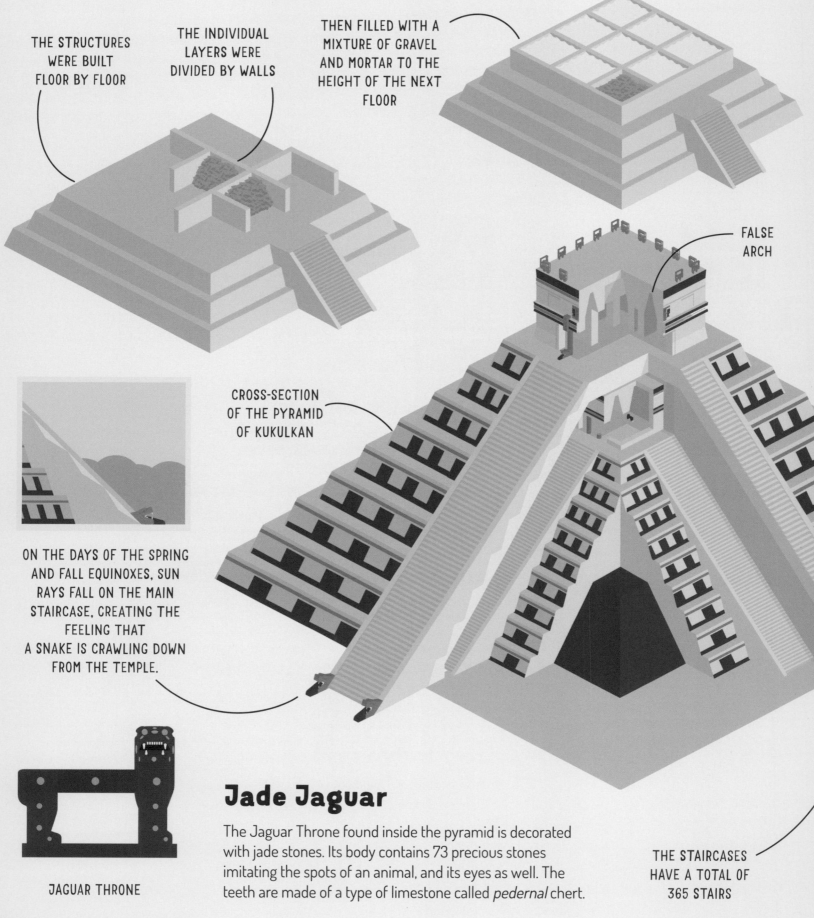

THE STRUCTURES WERE BUILT FLOOR BY FLOOR

THE INDIVIDUAL LAYERS WERE DIVIDED BY WALLS

THEN FILLED WITH A MIXTURE OF GRAVEL AND MORTAR TO THE HEIGHT OF THE NEXT FLOOR

FALSE ARCH

CROSS-SECTION OF THE PYRAMID OF KUKULKAN

ON THE DAYS OF THE SPRING AND FALL EQUINOXES, SUN RAYS FALL ON THE MAIN STAIRCASE, CREATING THE FEELING THAT A SNAKE IS CRAWLING DOWN FROM THE TEMPLE.

THE STAIRCASES HAVE A TOTAL OF 365 STAIRS

JAGUAR THRONE

Jade Jaguar

The Jaguar Throne found inside the pyramid is decorated with jade stones. Its body contains 73 precious stones imitating the spots of an animal, and its eyes as well. The teeth are made of a type of limestone called *pedernal* chert.

Workers

These majestic buildings were built for their rulers by thousands of farmers and herders. For the lower classes, this work was an obligation. The ruler of the city was titled *ahaw*.

THE HOUSING OF ORDINARY RESIDENTS WAS A LIGHTWEIGHT WOOD STRUCTURE COVERED BY STRAW

THE MATERIAL WAS CARRIED ON THE BACK IN A WOODEN CARRIER

Building Materials

Wood and heavy limestone for constructing the buildings were extracted on site and nearby so that they did not have to be transported in a complicated way. Workers carried other materials like lime for plastering and gypsum on their backs in special wooden harnesses like ones still used today.

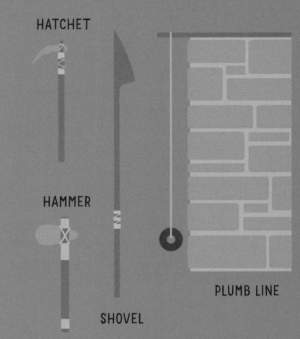

HATCHET

HAMMER

SHOVEL

PLUMB LINE

PRECISELY PROCESSED ON BLOCKS LAID DRY

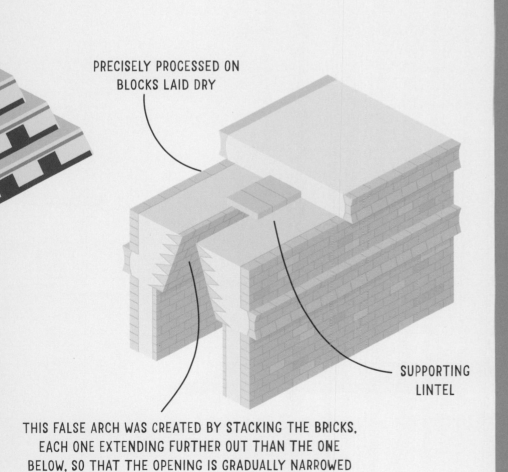

SUPPORTING LINTEL

THIS FALSE ARCH WAS CREATED BY STACKING THE BRICKS, EACH ONE EXTENDING FURTHER OUT THAN THE ONE BELOW, SO THAT THE OPENING IS GRADUALLY NARROWED

Construction Tools

The builders measured the area for construction using ropes of different lengths and plumb tools. They also used a water level and simple wooden tools, stones, and bones. In the later period, they used copper tools as well. For plastering the wall, stone or wooden tools similar to a trowel was used.

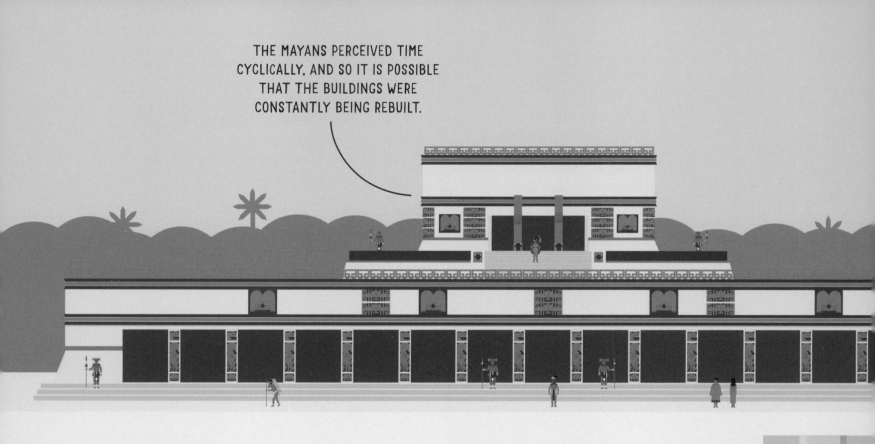

THE MAYANS PERCEIVED TIME CYCLICALLY, AND SO IT IS POSSIBLE THAT THE BUILDINGS WERE CONSTANTLY BEING REBUILT.

City Planning

Mayan cities were built according to a prearranged plan. The position of each temple, palace, square, and statue was planned in advance, as the city's plans were prepared exclusively by the priests based on their astronomical, cosmological, and religious knowledge and observations. The city was inhabited for hundreds of years and had many stages of development. The construction took place gradually, with the individual buildings having been under construction for decades.

Tzompantli

This is the original name for the ceremonial wall for hanging the heads and skulls of prisoners of war and ritual sacrifices. The wall of skulls located in Chichén Itzá, however, is not composed of real heads. The fake skulls are just for decoration.

TZOMPANTLI

Observatory

Another interesting building is the so-called Observatory, which has a dome-like roof that is not fully enclosed. It probably served Mayan astronomers observing the stars. However, since the Mayans did not have glass, they did not have telescopes. Astonishingly, everything they found in the sky, they observed with the naked eye.

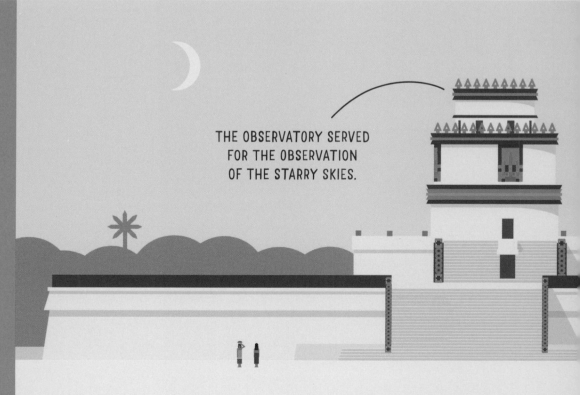

THE OBSERVATORY SERVED FOR THE OBSERVATION OF THE STARRY SKIES.

The Temple of the Warriors

Only a pyramid and forest of pillars remain of this large building today, thanks to which it is sometimes nicknamed the Hall of a Thousand columns. These columns supported the roof, which probably covered a space intended for religious assembly, or a marketplace. The temple was given its name for the figures of the warriors carved into the columns.

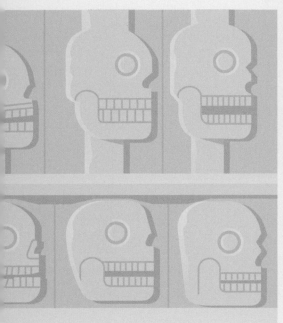

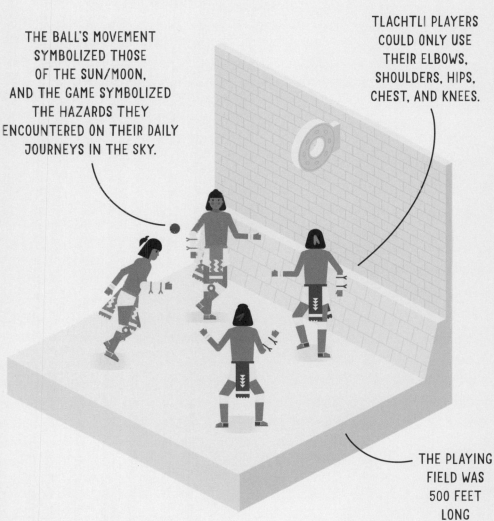

THE BALL'S MOVEMENT SYMBOLIZED THOSE OF THE SUN/MOON, AND THE GAME SYMBOLIZED THE HAZARDS THEY ENCOUNTERED ON THEIR DAILY JOURNEYS IN THE SKY.

TLACHTLI PLAYERS COULD ONLY USE THEIR ELBOWS, SHOULDERS, HIPS, CHEST, AND KNEES.

THE PLAYING FIELD WAS 500 FEET LONG

Tlachtli (Pok-a-tok)

The largest playing field for the game of tlachtli is located in Chichén Itzá. The aim was to get the ball to the end of the opponent's side, using your elbows, knees, and hips. The rules vary, and the losing side might have been sacrificed after losing the game! There are also theories that, on the contrary, the winners were the victims. These speculations, however, have never been confirmed.

Machu Picchu

In the language of the local Incas— the Quechua people—Machu Picchu means "Old Peak." At present, we use this name to refer to the ruins of the city located in the Peruvian part of the Andes Mountains. The name stuck because it was called that by the local farmer who helped an American explorer a century ago find the city.

Abandoned city

The Incas did not use letters in their written language, so no story from the city itself has been preserved. That's why the whole place is a mystery for scientists, and information about it are largely theoretical. Most theories are about the abandonment of the city. It is said that the population became extinct due to the epidemic brought by Spanish conquerors from Europe. Others claim that the locals were killed by neighboring tribes, or even killed each other. There is also a theory that the city was never completed and therefore was left uninhabited.

INTIHUATANA

MAIN TEMPLE

NOBLEWOMAN

QUEEN

PACHACUTI INCA YUPANQUI

Pachacuti Inca Yupanqui

Pachacuti Inca Yupanqui (1438–1472) is considered the founder of the city. He was the ninth ruler of the Inca Empire, which began building it before the mid-15th century. However, the city was abandoned after 100 years for as-yet unknown reasons. Although uninhabited and overgrown by the jungle, it was never truly forgotten by the locals.

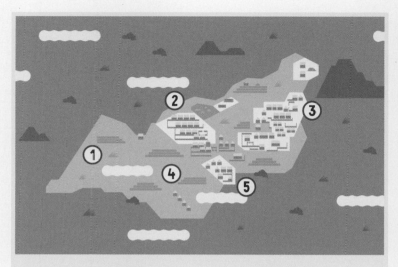

1. AGRICULTURE SECTION
2. SACRED DISTRICT
3. URBAN SECTION
4. TERRACES
5. ORDINARY BUILDINGS

WARRIOR

MERCHANT

LLAMA

Terraces

The terraces were built on steep slopes, due to its water retention and increased space for arable land. This way, the water would not flow down into the valley. It is believed that corn and potatoes were grown here. The individual terraces in the agricultural part are connected by stone stairs, and roughly 120 terraces are preserved here. Their height is not the same everywhere, but they reach up to 13 feet up.

What the Incas Used to Build

Peru is plagued by earthquakes, so to prevent the Incas' buildings from collapsing, mortar, which glues stones together, was not used. Instead, in the event of shockwaves, walls built without mortar can partially separate and then settle again without collapsing. Also, the roofs were built on a large slope of wood and covered with straw of the grass ichu, to better drain water and resist the wind.

SOIL

WATER CHANNEL

CROSS-SECTION OF THE TERRACE WALL

TERRACED GARDENS

STONE STAIRS

WOMAN WORKING WITH A HOE

CHAKITAQLLA—SIMPLE FOOT PLOW

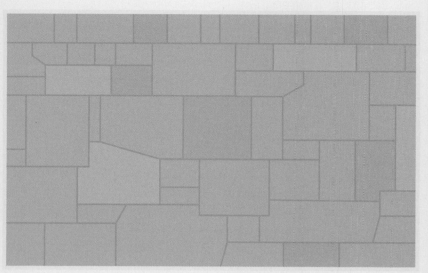

DETAIL OF THE WALL: THE GAPS BETWEEN THE STONES ARE SO TIGHT THAT NOT EVEN A SHEET OF PAPER CAN PASS THROUGH THEM.

Granite Blocks

All of the important structures were built by laying carved stones on top of each other. The big unknown is still how the Incas transported heavy granite blocks when they did not use wheels. Most likely by human force—dragging them on the ground, as evidenced by the number of scratches on the stones. The stone blocks were finally worked on site.

A HEIGHT UP TO 13 FEET

Agricultural Station

The city once served as a trial agricultural station where various types of crops were tested in different types of microclimates, due to the altitude. While this did not allow for large-scale cultivation, it let them grow a variety of crops.

Tools

The Incas used stone, wood, bone, and bronze tools for construction and agriculture. They had not discovered iron or the wheel—or at least, they did not use wheels for labor—and they worked the stones roughly in mines, similar to the technique used by Ancient Egyptians. The tool used to work the stone always had to be harder than the stone itself.

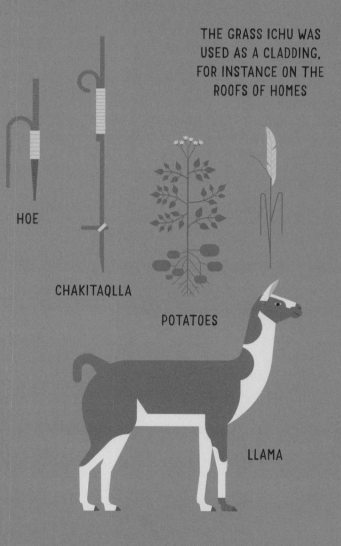

THE GRASS ICHU WAS USED AS A CLADDING, FOR INSTANCE ON THE ROOFS OF HOMES

HOE

CHAKITAQLLA

POTATOES

LLAMA

Llamas

Llamas were a very important animal for the Incas. They were beasts of burden and also a source of fur for making clothes. Even today, llamas help maintain the appearance of the ruins by grazing on the surrounding grass.

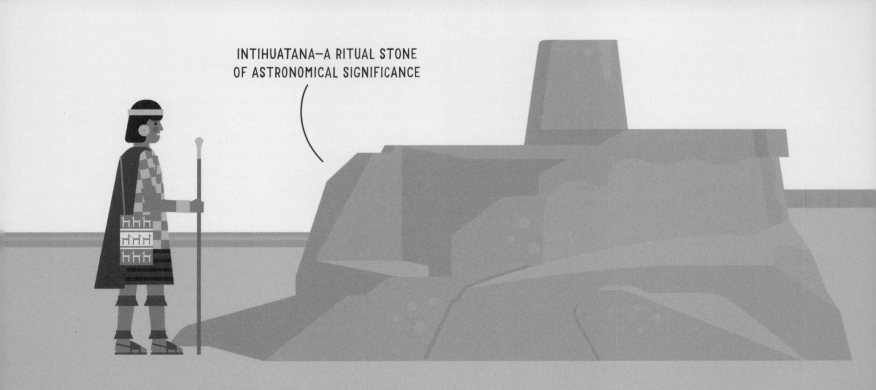

INTIHUATANA—A RITUAL STONE
OF ASTRONOMICAL SIGNIFICANCE

VIRACOCHA THE ALL-CREATOR,
ONE OF THE HOLIEST INCA GODS,
IS CONNECTED WITH THE OCEAN
AS THE GIVER OF LIFE.

Virgins of the Sun

The purpose of the construction is uncertain, mainly because we have no written records from the Inca Empire before Christopher Columbus's arrival in the Americas. The most widespread theory considers the city a sacred place of birth for Inca women, called "Virgins of the Sun."

VIRGIN OF THE SUN

PRIEST

MAIN TEMPLE

Hiram Bingham

Machu Picchu was already known in the 19th century, as evidenced by the atypical food remnants (peach stones, cow bones) found there then. The city is even marked on the maps from this time. However, the traveler, historian, and amateur archeologist Hiram Bingham was credited with raising awareness of the city on July 24, 1911. The route along the Urubamba River and a luxury train of the company Peru Rail is also named for him. The famous discoverer became the model for the well-known movie character Indiana Jones.

Artifacts

During his expedition, Bingham gathered large quantities of artifacts (bones, metal objects, ceramics), which he later took to Yale University in the USA. These objects are disputed by the Peruvian government, which to this day requests they be returned.

HIRAM BINGHAM

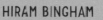

STORAGE CONTAINER

VASE

WAR AXE

Holy Site

The site was selected for building a city with sacred elements in the landscape, such as mountains, which are supposedly in harmony with key astrological events of the Incas. It is possible that the city also served as the seat of the Inca rulers.

City Districts

The ruins are spread over approximately 5 square miles and can be divided into two parts separated by a wall. The urban part is divided by a large square into the eastern and western parts. It is further divided into three districts. In the most important district—the sacred district—they built the Temple of the Sun (Intihuatana) and the Temple (Room) of the Three Windows, all of which were probably dedicated to the sun god, Inti. According to legend, he was a descendant of Viracocha the All-Creator. This entire district held a deep religious significance with the Inca.

ALTHOUGH THE CITY HAD NO COMMERCIAL OR MILITARY SIGNIFICANCE, THE INCAS HAD A LARGE ARMY WHOSE MEMBERS ENJOYED A HIGH SOCIAL STATUS.

The Taj Mahal

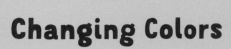
The Taj Mahal is a monumental Indian memorial (mausoleum) in Agra in the State of Uttar Pradesh in India, on the bank of the sacred Jamuna River. The Muslim mogul Shah Jahan had it built in memory of his wife Mumtaz Mahal, who died young. For many people, the Taj Mahal has become the symbol of all of India.

MUMTAZ MAHAL

Shah Jahan and Mumtaz Mahal

Shah Jahan and Mumtaz Mahal had 14 children together: eight sons and six daughters. However, when the last child was born in 1631, Mumtaz died at only 36 years old. The ruler had a state of mourning declared—for two long years, entertainment was forbidden. He promised to build a monument truly worthy of her memory and which no building in the world could match. He allegedly planned to build an identical copy of the mausoleum in black marble for himself, but the plan fell through due to a coup d'état led by his son. Shah Jahan was imprisoned and buried after his death next to his deceased wife.

Changing Colors

The mausoleum changes color—or at least appears to—due to the changing light of the day. It's pink in the morning, milky white in the evening, and if moonbeams fall on it, it turns gold. During the day, however, it looks like this.

OFFICER OF THE
MUGHAL ARMY WITH
A BIRD OF PREY

ROYAL GUARD OF
EMPEROR SHAH JAHAN

THE TAJ MAHAL IS ONE OF THE MOST FAMOUS BUILDINGS OF MUGHAL ARCHITECTURE

1. MOSQUE
2. POOLS
3. TOMB / MAUSOLEUM
4. GUEST HOUSE
5. TAJ MAHAL
6. MAIN GATE

EMPEROR SHAH JAHAN

TOMB OF MUMTAZ MAHAL

THE PREDOMINANT MOTIF OF IRISES

Material

The marble that the Taj Mahal is built from comes from Rajasthan, the jasper from Indian Punjab, the jade and crystal from China, the turquoise from Nepal, and the lazurite from Afghanistan. Sapphire was imported from Sri Lanka and carnelian from Arabia.

White Marble

White marble was brought to the construction site from a quarry more than 150 miles away. Its carving is very complicated, and the details are especially impressive. The large number of elaborate decorations showcases the precise craftsmanship of the builders.

Pietra Dura

This technique comes from Italy and is a form of inlaying. A pattern is engraved into the marble or another foundation, and the hole is then filled with another stone or mosaic, thus creating the pattern. In the case of the Taj Mahal, these are ornaments and mostly floral motifs that can be seen in the palace in a thousand different forms.

MANY SMALL PROCESSED STONES FORMING ORNAMENTS ARE SET INTO THE MARBLE

Mughal Empire

The Mughals were Muslims who ruled India and Pakistan in the 16th and 17th centuries. During their reign, the area changed considerably, which impacted architecture, among other things. The Taj Mahal was the pinnacle of Mughal architecture, which rivaled that of Persian, Islamic, and original Hindu buildings.

MALIK AMBAR—THE LEADER WHO BECAME FAMOUS IN THE BATTLES AGAINST MUGHAL TROOPS.

MUGHAL SOLDIER

LADY-IN-WAITING

ENTRANCE TO THE TOMB

ELEPHANTS WERE
ALSO USED TO
TRANSPORT MATERIALS

Elephants

Because of their strength and size, elephants were used in the Mughal army. Protected by armor, they were almost invincible. Some even had chained tusks and were the key to the success of the Mughal army, and therefore the entire Mughal Empire. The elephant force was also used outside of combat—in transport and construction. The material for constructing the Taj Mahal traveled to Agra from all over Asia and was transported by more than 1,000 elephants.

Paradise on Earth

It is said that the whole complex was designed as an earthly replica of a house of paradise, like the idea of Muslim paradise. The main building has perfect marble cladding, which is inlaid using a special technique with semi-precious stones such as jade, jasper, turquoise, and crystal to create its beautiful decorative motifs. As such, it showcases the refined aesthetics that peaked during the reign of Shah Jahan. The Taj Mahal thus today remains one of the most elegant, most harmonious, and most symmetrical buildings in the world. It is an example of the wealth and eccentricity of Mughal art and architecture.

MINARETS

Entrance to Paradise

The Taj Mahal lies in the middle of extensive gardens, which are entered through a large decorated entrance gate, which symbolizes the entrance to paradise.

MAIN GATE

BIBI KA MAQBARA

Other Tombs

Another building miles away belongs indirectly to this breathtaking marble tomb. It is another unique tomb, which almost copies the Taj Mahal. It is called the Bibi Ka Maqbara. Azam Shah had this building constructed from 1657 to 1661 for his mother. It is a slightly smaller, less ostentatious replica of the Taj Mahal.

A Smaller Tomb

Another substantially smaller tomb, I'timād-ud-Daulah, was built one sovereign generation earlier and might have served as a template for the Taj Mahal.

I'TIMĀD-UD-DAULAH

Christ the Redeemer

The Statue of Christ the Redeemer (*Cristo Redentor* in Portuguese) stands on the peak of Corcovado Mountain (2,340 feet above sea level), towering over the Brazilian city of Rio de Janeiro.

1. MARACANÃ STADIUM
2. STATUE OF THE CHRIST
3. CORCOVADO MOUNTAIN
4. PORT OF RIO DE JANEIRO
5. SUGARLOAF MOUNTAIN
6. COPACABANA BEACH

Designers

Back in 1859, the priest Pedro Maria Boss decided on the position of the statue, suggesting it to the Brazilian Princess Isabella. Engineer Heitor da Silva Costa then laid the cornerstone in 1922, and in 1923 a competition was finally held to pick the right statue. The winning design depicted Jesus with arms outstretched, symbolically embracing and protecting the city. The work itself began in 1926. However, the final form is the work of a French sculptor of Polish descent: Paul Landowski.

ONE HAND WEIGHTS EIGHT TONS

HEITOR
DA SILVA COSTA

PAUL LANDOWSKI

RIO DE JANEIRO
BRAZIL

1922

Chapéu do Sol

An observation point called Chapéu do Sol (meaning "sun hat") originally stood on the top of the mountain. It earned its name for its shape. Pedro II, the last Brazilian emperor, had it built, along with what was the first tourist railway in South America.

A Concrete Cross

Artist Carlos Oswald first came up with the idea that the statue itself should have the shape of a cross. But the shape of outstretched arms creates structural problems. To support them, Silva decided to use what was then "the material of the future"—concrete.

A Statue of Reinforced Steel

Other than the outer layers, the statue is made of reinforced concrete. For the outside, the designer Heitor da Silva Costa chose soapstone (steatite), a material with enduring qualities that is easy to work. The statue is 98 feet high and stands on an octagonal black-granite pedestal 25 feet high. The distance between outstretched arms is 75 feet. The whole statue weighs about 700 tons.

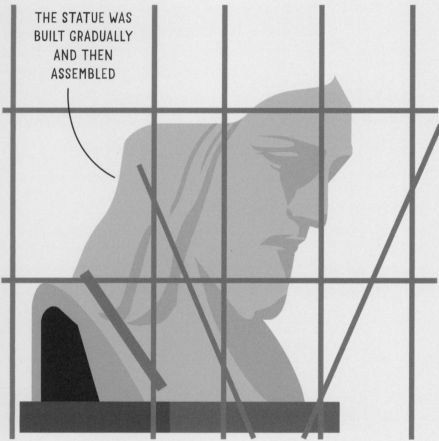

THE STATUE WAS BUILT GRADUALLY AND THEN ASSEMBLED

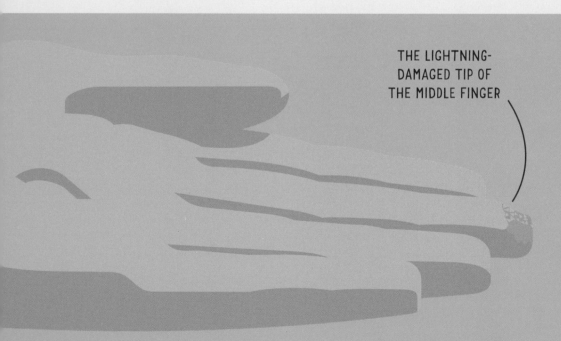

THE LIGHTNING-DAMAGED TIP OF THE MIDDLE FINGER

Damaged by Lightning

In 2008 and again in 2014, the statue was damaged by lightning, requiring partial repairs. Every year, the statue is hit by two to four bolts of lightning, but most fortunately don't cause any damage. For protection, the statue has a steel lightning rod on its head in the form of an inconspicuous "crown of thorns" from which the steel ropes lead over both hands to the ground, where they are grounded.

REINFORCED CONCRETE
CONSTRUCTION

EXAMPLE OF
A MOSAIC

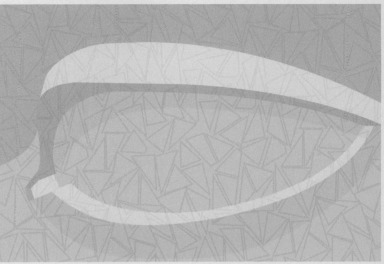

THE LAST TWO
FLOORS

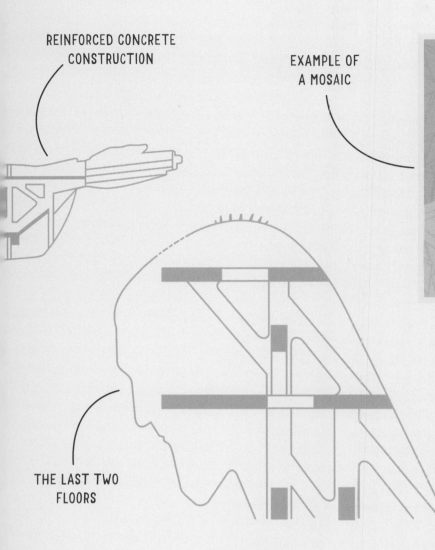

ONE OF THE FIVE
HOLES IN THE
STATUE

Materials

The original technical plan provided for the creation of a steel structure in the shape of a cross. But this didn't work, so it was replaced by reinforced concrete. As a mosaic, they then added pieces of soapstone, which is better and easier to work with. In the long run, it's more stable than other materials and gives the statue its trademark white color.

The Inside of the Statue

Inside the Christ, reinforced beams form 12 floors connected by a staircase. The tenth floor is at the level of the hands, and the last two floors are in the head. Five holes in the statue are used to access its surface. One of them is at the head, two on the shoulders, and two at the elbows.

Warmed by the Sun

The statue of Christ deliberately faces east. Silva wanted the statue to be the first sunlit and visible object in the city. Likewise at sunset, when a halo appears around his head, in a sense telling the city good night. One hand also points north, and the other south. Because it is an unmissable icon, it significantly helps tourists orient themselves in the city.

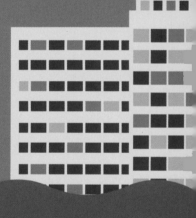

THE STATUE OF CHRIST

REAL ESTATE PRICES IN RIO DE JANEIRO GO UP IF THE STATUE OF CHRIST CAN BE SEEN FROM THE WINDOW.

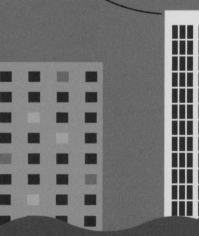

Art Deco

Art Deco is a visual style from the early 20th century that influenced architecture, fashion, and also art. The statue of Christ is designed in this artistic style.

WOMEN'S FASHION
1920s

MEN'S FASHION
1920s

CAR FROM THE EARLY
20th CENTURY

Facing the City

Nevertheless, the monument has been criticized for facing the rich and luxurious districts of Rio, with its back turned on the poor quarter—the favelas.

Sightseeing train

A train track leads to the mountaintop. Built in 1884, it ends, however, 130 feet below the peak. From the final stop onward, a footpath, consisting of 220 steps, continues to the base of the statue. An observation deck stands on the statue's pedestal. The construction went hand in hand with the project to construct special train tracks to the top of the mountain.

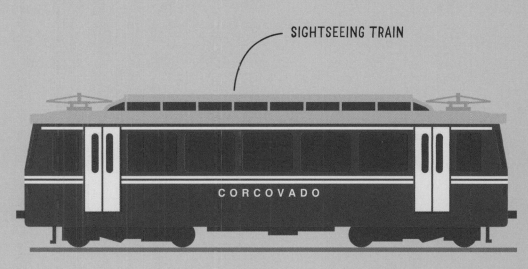

SIGHTSEEING TRAIN

CORCOVADO

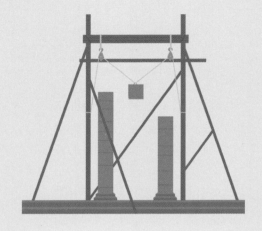

© B4U Publishing for Albatros,
an imprint of Albatros Media Group, 2023
5. května 1746/22, Prague 4, Czech Republic
Authors: Jiří Bartůněk, Tom Velčovský
Illustrator: Jan Šrámek
Translator: Sean Mark Miller, MA
Editor: Scott Alexander Jones

www.albatrosbooks.com